WHAT WE TURNED INTO

WHAT WE TURNED INTO

ARROW BRAKE

Library of Congress Control Number:		2022905286
ISBN:	Hardcover	978-1-6698-1716-1
	Softcover	978-1-6698-1715-4
	eBook	978-1-6698-1714-7

Print information available on the last page.

Rev. date: 03/21/2022

To order additional copies of this book, contact:
Xlibris
844-714-8691
www.Xlibris.com
Orders@Xlibris.com
841362

Authors Note:

You are strong, you got this, and I believe in you.

~ Arrow

To the people who stay awake at night wondering why.

CONTENTS

Preface

This is the first book I have ever written which is composed of my poetry over the past three years telling my life story as I battle mental health issues. Living with the effects of traumatic experiences and mental illness can feel very isolating and like nobody understands through your perspective. My hope is through each poem someone who has had similar experiences is able to know they are not alone.

Introduction

Welp, I'm supposed to be dead. You might be wondering why I'm not and why I'm supposed to be, well I can answer that with this question; why does everything in life have a sequence of events? Everyone gets a different hand of cards dealt to them in life. Some people start with royal flush others don't even get the right amount of cards but somehow, someway you learn to work with what ya got. Even if it almost ends up killing you.

Think?

I just can't understand my thoughts if that makes sense, everything just swirls around like Earth on its axis making me live in my hell every day. I feel trapped; I just can't put my thoughts into words. I would say be me so you can understand but if I'm being real, what I say, what I feel it's all a lie. I can't hear my own thoughts there are too many at a time, but the shadow figures around me can help me figure them out, or wait, am I supposed to figure them out what even is it? A man, a woman, a person from my past? Or is it all of my thoughts in front of my face and I still can't make sense of it. If my thoughts could build a person what would they be? Strong, independent, brave, or free they would probably just reflect off of me, an empty shadow that has nothing more to give or be.

No light shines

Don't cut, don't cry, don't look at the crystals in my eyes. Don't weep, don't wallow, don't look at the darkness in the hollow. Suck it up, swallow, smile as you wallow. Don't let it show shove your feelings as you go. Slowly it will grow, that goes right down below, into the hollow where no light ever shows.

A will to death

Think when you're about to kill yourself, what would it do for you? Show how you really feel, or just prove the real you? The person who didn't know how to work it through and could only see one point of view. You never had a clue until you withdrew from everything you wanted to pursue. What are you going to do as you rot, just think of everything you got? A small casket with the belongings you wrote in your note as you held a knife at your throat so that way you can float as you quote everything you wrote in your note.

Why do you hate?

Why do I stay up throughout the night? Is it so I can write, out of spite, so I have the will to fight? I don't know how much longer I can put up with the pain every day, I just feel drained. Not because of my actions or what I have put on to myself, but what others have put me through. Sometimes it can be out of the blue and I know I'm screwed. They are always so crude and I wish they could be sued for all the things they have put me through. You don't know what it's like, try to take your life, wanting it to end. Knowing you could've been at your prime but you let others take your time on a dime knowing what they're doing is a hate crime.

Earth's blood

I don't want to have to deal with the hate that floods this Earth. No, I'm not selfish, I just don't care to relish in the sadness this world has to offer. Don't let this misguide you, the world can be a great place but for every face, there's a different race, that people just do not know how to embrace. light it on fire they said, the streets are filled with red. Don't forget your mask, by this point, I should just carry a flask. Watch the news they say, why so I can be filled with the blues? There are major problems in our world right now yes, it sure does help to keep me depressed. Everyone deals with their problems, the world just adds to them. If only there was some sort of split, where we could commit, to give the Earth, back its blood.

Them

Be honest, do you even love me, or do you love the fact that I'm your blood? I'm lost in the floods of my tears that you provoked just because you "misspoke." I wish I could make you proud so you could go and show your crowd but whatever I do it's wrong so for me to heal I sing a song. So that way I don't cut, but you say I just shut the world out. I want you to be happy but my happiness matters just as much as yours. I wish I could open the doors for you to see, why I want to be free. This is my plead, I'm tired of begging for your approval. This is so brutal, yet I still put up with it because in some sort of way I still love you. I just wish you knew how much I grew, how far I flew, and what I have gone through for you to understand, why I want to be free from this mental prison you have sentenced me to.

Bloodstained tears

Close the door. Close the door. I want to hear no more, for there is a roar that is signaling a war. I'm already in enough pain itself. I'm mentally exhausted all the time, which makes me feel like I'm a mime when I want to scream but I don't know how. Waking up in a sweat, hoping that I do not regret. I've been waking up earlier so I can decide what shirt best covers my arms, for I have created many harms that heald me while I feel to sleep. I'm trying hard to stop, but if I don't I will cry till I have no air left in my soul that used to once be full. You cover up so people don't see the truth, they'll just blame it on your youth. They don't know what's going on, they don't care to look upon how I've mentally aged myself and that I now sit on a shelf with the rest of their "trophies." When I try to explain all I obtain is pain from people who are too vain and do not know how to retain. I sit in bed and count the time as I feel like a mime, wondering if the cuts get deeper over time.

I matter?

Some days I feel like a porcelain doll, made out of glass that people like to harass. They don't like it that I don't sit still and talk. I am watched like a hawk. They're scared that I am my own person and not their pretty doll they can control. At this point, I am digging a hole. Dress like a girl so that way you can twirl. Do what you're told, Smile, Walk with grace, change your face. Nobody wants an ugly doll, if you don't, you will fall. People need to be around other humans, for they need their light. I've been trying to count my lumens, but there's not many, so I'm left in the dark where all I can think of are marks. I'm hurt by people pretending like they care when they don't. They say they won't when you tell them not to leave you in the dark, I am tired of having marks from trying to escape my dark. I'm trying to tell myself that I only need me out of 7.8 billion I'm getting tired of being a civilian. I know that I am more and that I want to explore this vase world that surrounds me and 7.8 billion. I don't want to be a pretty doll that does when I'm told, but at the same time, I don't think I can shapeshift from what I have already become because I am a figure made out of glass that people like to harass. The glass from my body drips with tears as I am living through my fears, but glass from my body has been shattered, all the pieces are scattered, the glass from my body won't stick together, I am made like a feather. I am not a porcelain doll but the world controls. I feel earth souls breaking the glass so that I can't walk with grace, just don't look at my face. I don't do what I'm told for I am bold and I will not be controlled. I will not have my soul sold because I am made of gold out of 7.8 billion I may just be a civilian, but if there's anything I know about this vast world is that I am not a porcelain doll that people can control because I have a goal, to pick up the glass from my body that has been shattered and battered, even though the pieces are scattered, I make my way back through the cracks where blood sometimes runs from me trying to find more lumens as I can't connect with other humans.

Not my father

Well dad I'm now sixteen, why didn't you ever intervene? I know you and mom are no longer together, but that shouldn't make it so I have to act like leather, tough-looking on the outside, but easy to tear and fragile on the inside. I've never had a guide which sometimes made me feel like I died, all because you got rid of me for another woman. I feel like the last omen, the last trace of any sort of blood that bonds, I can't help but wonder what my life would be like if I ever heard you respond. Next year I'll be seventeen, eighteen, then finally an adult that you no longer have to pay child support on so you can leave your ex-wife in the dust. Everything you have done is a disgust. Don't you ever wonder what goes on in my life, I do for you. I wish I could ask you how your day at work was. I've wished you were there to teach me how to drive. I wish you were there when I tried to kill myself and wipe my tears as I am engulfed with my fears. You never have and you never will be there for me. All this time I thought something was wrong with me because you left but the real reason was that you are a theft. You never told the truth, which made my trust issues start young. I should have realized everything you said was all wrapped up under your tongue.

Blanket of secrecy

1, 2, 3, 4 I can't do this anymore. 5, 6, 7, 8, should I hesitate or should I just try to meditate? The past two months have really changed my life. I no longer have access to knives. Thought I had it. I gave in. One morning I got up and started walking towards a bridge thinking how long is it going to take till I jump and how loud will the thump of my body be as it hits the tracks so I can finally relax. I had a friend who saved my life. I bet I got a million calls from her after I sent her a text telling her goodbye, knowing that I was going to die as tears came flooding to my eyes, but I am still here and I am still living. I am still breathing. I am alive and I will survive. I'm still not completely sure if I'm going to thrive but at least I'm alive. I went and I dived into this thing we call life beautiful, miserable, blissful, nonaccepting, heartbreaking, beautiful life. Maybe it's a good thing I have no more knives so I can try to find this thing called life.

Visions

Recently I've been thinking about my future because I keep telling myself I'm going to live till then I remember when I was ten, I wanted to be a paleontologist because I was so interested in the past, but now I'll do whatever it takes to escape it. I want to be able to help people through my writing so they can keep on fighting. I suppress too much of what I feel, which makes me go back to the past where I remember how much I have been harassed. When I was thirteen, I wanted to be the police so I can make sure no one gets hurt like I have been, then my mind goes back to when I was ten, and a part of me gets sad knowing I will never be a child again. Through my sixteen years, I feel like I've lived a thousand. I read a quote once that said "his skin and clothes were torn apart from centuries of torment" which made me think about my arms and all the harms I have created and how much I have been hated, not just by others, but by myself, which makes my mind trace back to when I tried to hang myself from a shelf. People are going to hate on you all the time you can't change that, but what you can change is the hatred you give to yourself. What doesn't help is when you hang yourself from a shelf and leave this earth without knowing your worth. People will hate, people will hit, people will spit in your face and tell you that you are worthless but what you have to do is don't walk towards a shelf but find your worth and know that you have earned your place on this Earth because survival is not for the weak, it's for those who are able to speak hope and worth and find their place on this Earth.

Flashlight

Are you alive? You probably answered yes because you are breathing and your body is here, but where is your mind? Do you feel like your life is defined? Anymore it seems like the world is being replaced by its shadow. A blanket of secrecy is how I define it. How do you define the world that surrounds you? Is it truly your view? Do you know what's true to you? The world is covered in a blanket of secrets for as long as I have known, maybe that's part of the reason I feel so alone. I've been asked, what do I think of the world before, I then also thought of mine and how I made the two worlds combine. If there's one thing anybody could ever learn from me is don't let others' problems become yours. Don't become another problem in our world. Don't become a problem in your world. Learn how to make things not swirled. I let my pain take me away in the shadow. I soon became numb and everything became blurred. This is my attempt to be heard, not slurred or attacked. My life will no longer be cracked. My legs and lungs were straining there was so much darkness I didn't know where to run except to a knife where I almost took my life. Was I getting from my straining? No, I wasn't. I didn't realize that in the darkness when there is no light, you can make your own just like how they invented the flashlight. I took that light and I shined it towards hope, so that way I can cope instead of going towards a knife trying to take my life when all I ended up gaining was scars but in the darkness I found stars. I'm looking forward to a life with no more knives.

Fight

The softest started strongest. Why do you think they last the longest? The ones that are weak turned the warriors. Why is that? Because of the ones that start off soft start off scared. We don't want to be compared. Everyone tries to win the war. Everyone tries to be more, but in order to be more, you have to win the war. Everyone says that time changes you. I don't think that's true. It's the flashbacks and pain you know it's not all in your brain, but when you try to explain all you gain is more pain. I wasn't prepared for the war, which left me soft and scared. I thought people cared. I soon realized you only have yourself at the end of the day, you can't let yourself go away. You have to learn how to fight and not be engulfed in fright. You have to find your light so you can win the war so you can be more.

Dispel

You can't stop what's coming. To live your heaven you must live your life. Don't live your life with a knife or scream under your smile, sit back, wait awhile. When two fronts become one, you see life and a new frame. The lenses are a bit blurry, but that's because you were in a hurry. Don't scream under your smile, sit back, wait awhile. When you're sitting in that new frame, look far out. View the details of that picture not the ones with a hundred billion of a girl thrown away by the world that could have been pearled. Feel hell burning under your skin, let it within. Take a walk through hell, ring the bell, let it dispel so that way when you were looking through the lenses they aren't blurry because you weren't in a hurry you allowed yourself to feel your hell so you could dispel.

I'm a writer

Be a victim or a fighter. I find those words circling my head, maybe that's why I'm not dead because I chose to be a fighter. Or did I choose to be a writer? You can be alone and surrounded by violence. You can be alone and have nothing but fear to keep you company. You can choose to be a victim or a fighter, or maybe even a writer. When I started writing, I never thought I could help anybody, not even myself. I was lost in the constant darkness of being a victim I didn't know choosing to be a fighter was an option, but you have a choice you have a voice, use it and speak up for what is right and fight. Don't go into a flight because when you run from your problems, you then don't have a choice because you lost your voice. It's not pain, it's power. You are becoming a tower, soon you'll be able to look down on who and what's hurt you because you are now above that. To get out, you need to look in and fight, because when you run from what's hurting you soon you lose your voice. Be a victim or fighter, I chose to become a writer. My tower is still building because I'm still healing. I rather be dealing and fight, than go into a flight because now I have a choice because I found my voice.

Andromeda & Milky way

I'm tired, I'm happy, I'm miserable, but I'm not. I feel everywhere and nowhere at the same time. It all fits into a rhyme. One where you can and can't feel the effects of time, you've committed a crime. You lost yourself in the vanishing point. You can't see yourself in time and you can't feel yourself in space. I don't want to look at my face. I see multiple images in one in a broken mirror, is it my face or space? Through the broken pieces of time all you can do is try to live out your crime I'm lost in the vanishing point where there is no time or space and somehow, someway I'm still trying to figure out my place.

Rebound?

Why? Why Am I down and out, laying on the floor crying, eyes red and shirt wet from getting dirty water dumped on me. I don't know how long I will be down here, but I will rise again. I know you're supposed to look over the past so you can see your future, but what happens when there's a loud sudden noise and you're taken back, down on the ground, and you have to figure out how to rebound. Everyone says adulting is the hardest part, but I haven't made it to that point yet, instead, I've been training in a battlefield of brick walls and tiled floors, learning to use my peripheral vision to see if someone's behind me, figuring out body movements and tone of voice along with looking to see if hands out of pockets at all times. My innocence was taken like a dime sold for ten cents sporadically throughout time as I lost more of my dimes. Now I might not be an adult, but that does not mean I'm at fault. I may know a thing or two, blood is red and the sky is blue, life doesn't have to be through. You may be down and out, eyes red and shirt wet, but you're not their pet. I may not be an adult, but I do know a thing or two. Bullies will push you down and drown you in dirty water making your shirt wet, so you can be their pet. You may be down on the ground but you have to figure out how to rebound because life will not wait, You cannot hesitate. Do not be someone's pet. You will drown and end up on the ground. It's your choice to rebound.

Why didn't you call?

Anymore I'm hanging on by a thread wondering when I'm going to be dead. I'm not sure if I want to live I've already died, it's been implied. When I reach out to the future, all I see is pain, but I have a great life. Isn't that right? I have tangible items and a bed to sleep in, but what about those things that aren't tangible? Friends, family, someone that actually wants to be around you. Money can't buy happiness, know why because tangible items can't laugh with you, spend time with you or be there when you want to cut the loneliness away so you have to portray because when you don't and let down your walls you will get into brawls. After all, you have tangible items and a bed to sleep in. You should be happy your life isn't crappy. You have a knife to cut the loneliness away. Everything will be okay. No text, no calls. So I build up my walls and watch as I fall wishing someone would have called.

Interconnection

There's a connection to the mirror when it's broken has it really spoken? Only showing your reflection in pieces as your self esteem decreases. If you could reassemble the glass, would it make your world vaster, but hasn't the mirror already spoken telling you that you're broken? So what good would it do reassembling the glass trying to make your world more vast if you're only ever going to see your reflection in pieces so your self esteem decreases. You pick up the glass trying to reassemble, but instead, your arms start to tremble. Your self esteem drips away at the sound of water running as you look in the mirror and see your reflection and pieces as your self-esteem increases, you pick up the glass and throw it away. Your reflection should be on display because you've made it to today the mirror has spoken and you are not broken. You tried to reassemble the glass and that's all the mirror could ask. When you look at your reflection, you'll see an interconnection, not to the mirror or its glass, but because you've surpassed from the trembling and started reassembling.

What's happiness?

What's the point in happiness? Why not live your life in sappiness? Well, today I got that answer. It's sitting with your friends while laughing, not crying. You sit there for a moment and don't feel like dying. The loneliness went away for a bit, I'm scared about the hit. When reality comes back and I'm reminded of what I lack. I'm just grateful the world cut me some slack.

Roshan

Mustn't I lay here begrimed knowing I've lost out on time. To lay like a whale at bay as I feel myself to decay. Wondering the feeling of swimming in the ocean with no nets or regrets as people forget about the sailor once out among the ocean filled with roshan that soon got stolen as people forgot and the boat crashed. No one seemed to care about the splash, so the sailor sat there and cried, feeling begrimed wishing that people paid more time instead they threw out nets tricking you until you sink, but somehow you swam back up to roshan until you got caught in people's nets, which made you filled with regrets. Just wanting to swim again.

Alone.

How can one feel the breeze when they haven't felt the dirt? How can one feel the warmth of the ocean water without feeling the scorching sand under their feet? Sometimes you have to brace the scorching sand to feel the warm ocean water. Sometimes you have to walk through the dark to find a light other times you have to make your own, which can make you feel alone.

Red leaves

Yesterday I walked through the woods with a blade in my pocket thinking of where I should slit my wrist. Sitting on the bench under the tree with the red leaves blowing in the splotches of sunlight under the trees like splotches of blood on the sleeve of my hoodie as I try not to just hide the pain from everyone, but also to myself from the pain that confides. I know where it resides or lack of wording where it hides. I've been trying to do more writing or more blunt way of saying it, keep on fighting. You are probably wondering why didn't you do it, and honestly, I don't know. As I pulled the blade out from my pocket with the dry blood still on it as the fall sunlight beamed off of it, which forced my head to turn the other way as my eyes fell upon the tree with red leaves that floated to the ground with the crunch, which reminded me of two things. One is that being human can sometimes feel like being a leaf. You tear easily and when you fall to the ground people can sometimes step on you, but the other is being a leaf can be beautiful some can be multicolored. There is beauty in everything and where there is beauty there can sometimes be pain which is a trick from your brain that the pain will remain and can make you feel insane and you don't know where to begin to explain. If you're anything like me, it's lead you to a blade and with every cut I made I felt like I had the answers to restrain from the pain that confides that I forced myself to hide, which lead me to the woods where I saw this tree with the red leaves which reminded me for times filled with nothing but pain, you have to keep trying to push through and find the beauty, even in the smallest of things like multicolored leaves, which in my eyes symbolize happiness.

Tornado of fire

Is it my fault or his? Some people disagree and then the fault falls back on me. I don't know what to write, what to say besides the presence of dismay. The first time took my virginity the second gave me the lesson of fear and the third showed me what it feels like to be nobody, took my pride, told me to no one must I confide. Everything was frozen in the light of fire as violence was sung as at first, the fire was not in sight, there were no clue of future freights. Until one day the small twig snapped and emerged was an inferno inside the fiery hell used to once be this little girl full of pride that got taken away as kumbaya was sung one, two, three how many more will there be? Struggling for her sanity as the inferno spun with abuse death by a thousand cuts that thought rained red blood in the mix of a fiery hell. As blood turned blacked and tears started to burn, hoping that it would have helped the inferno turn back into the fire that used to once burn. Violence danced as kumbaya was sung, the inferno twirled to the Symphony of abuse. The little girl whose face was broken her body replaced with rags and scars as she watched herself burn in hell, knowing there is no escape as she watched herself burn she soon hope someday she becomes an urn as she wishes a silent secret, for him to burn alongside her.

Fear

An ode to fear. What all do you hear? Silent cries in the nights filled with freights from the future and past, where everything becomes amassed.

To my fears, what all do you hear? Screams from abusers that I now know are all users or the ocean waves being pulled by the moon, filled with tears of a monsoon.

To my fears please tell me what you hear, the sound of my heart feeling like it's going to give, telling me I have nothing more to live.

To all my fears, you may not tell me what you hear, but I would like to say thank you for keeping me near. Even if one day I disappear, I hope by then I'll be able to tell what you hear.

A.B.A.B (always been a boy)

I want to cry but I know it's not my time for I have to complete this rhyme, a rhyme lost in time. I look in the mirror and I see a model but not the kind you would think, the kind with long blonde hair that will give you a wink more or less so a boy with the wisdom of a man pale skin with short dark hair that's always so fluffy it's hard to be styled. Organized but yet still erratic, some people say he would look better in an attic. Locked away from the normals, the conformed robots of society. Under his clothes, his body doesn't portray who he is with curves and breasts that confine to his chest, that he hides while he binds, hoping to be seen as a normal. A forbidden model that the perception of normal has vanished. He sits in his room as the numbing fades and he starts to feel, hoping one day he'll be able to heal for the man knows it's not his time as the boy tries to complete the rhyme, the rhyme lost in time.

Pinocchio

I feel like Pinocchio, not because I'm a liar, I want to be a real boy too and not controlled by the strings of what we call society. In a sense, I feel like I'm a liar and I'm not sure why. Maybe it's my binder under my shirt that I've casually try to fix as I feel like my spine is going to snap, liar. Or my shaky voice as I fight back tears, liar. I tell myself it's going to get better as my blankets tie my legs to my bed, holding my head, wondering at the sunrise will be any different. Dreams and visions of a life that could be mine or should have been, count the ten, hold your breath, nothing more will lie after death. Sticks and stones can break my bones but words will never hurt me, as my wooden arms get pulled by the strings. Tell me what you bring, life is not meant for "my kind" people treat you like an "it" a non-human creepy creature walking near their children as parents pull them away or in school hallways as people laugh and whisper slurs but words will never hurt me, right? A wooden boy living in a world meant for "real men". Count to ten, hold your breath, would life get better after death? A wooden boy whose strings make his nose grow. How dare he cut the strings and be himself? I don't want to be placed on a shelf. Brave and true, something of that of a fairy who's blue. A real boy, he is who? Brave and selfless and true too maybe not to you, but to himself. He will not be placed on a shelf.

Burning Branches

When I was a child, I used to go to the forest and jump over the branches. Now I smoke the leaves and watch as my problems float away as I strayed from the reality, the absence of my mortality. Growing up in a world full of smoke, where everything is just a joke and you never make it to jump over the branches again. Lungs on fire, brain broken of wires, to be young and dumb they say I have problems, I watch them float away. Too young to have problems, to old to know how the world works. Problems, don't worry, they lurk. Soon to be seventeen, head in the clouds and hard to breathe. Anxiety from society in the absence of sobriety. As I watch my problems float, I reminisce that of a quote, to the child that used to once live in reality with no thoughts of mortality's, no issues to cope, not doin' dope, jumping over the branches, a smile that used to once take place.

Windows

Windows as big as the moon, my eyes, they gloom, sunlight shines through. Green as the trees swaying in the breeze, the moon shines bright a light in the night through the window where dust falls an empty soul left to call.

Him

Why does it still hurt? I lay in bed remembering what you said the day you told me I would never be a man. Some pain is indescribable. Some pain is unimaginable. Some pain will make you drive unaware of the destination but knowing you have to leave. Anymore I don't have the words, lately the tears either, science is facts, but as you attack then retract the things you said as I held my head in the car crying as my soul was dying. You say I'm just not complying. What is there to comply with a person's soul they are who they are whole but apparently, that's not you. You fell through of what made you a man. You said things without a plan as you took your brother's soul with each dagger in disguise as words. You cut my heart in thirds.

Glue

Rivers and streams. Shallow seas, to my inadequate we disagree. I catch my breath as I descend, is that honestly what you meant to intend? Blood pumps from my heart to my veins that end up leaving stains. In the light of the moon, blood shines through, grab some glue put yourself back together no one is going to do that for you. Look at it as bad or good. Life is like glue, It's all in your point of view. Do you view life as sticky and a mess, or look at it as a tool to put yourself where you deserve.

For who?

A father can be many things in one, a father points a gun, but to whom? Out in the open to defend his family or take that gun as one to defend himself. A daughter who is his son, the son who is or isn't his sun. Who for he has a gun but for whom? People take things as they assume. The spring before summer, they bloom. They spin into the yard with the mystery not yet in the mind of conscious. Soon to be disconcerted for now everything is covered but to whom? everything will be seen as you assume.

"Superman"

I'm not a man, I'm just a boy. He used my heart like a toy. My first love, I felt like I was floating above. I asked if it was just me and then I remember how we kissed under the tree. A tear falls from my eye as I start to cry. "I'm in it for the long run," I said you said "I don't know if I can commit", which makes me question if I'll ever be the right fit. The first time I ever said I love you I said I hate you because love scared me and it still does but you laughed with that beautiful smile and I knew I would be staying for a while, but it must have never really been that way for you since you said you can't commit, I think I know why I'm not the right fit. I asked the hard questions first and with how you looked, I should have known you wouldn't stay. I know you said it doesn't, but I feel like it does. It bothers you that I'm not cis but as we kissed that one night, you did a twist as you stopped moving your hand down my leg but to my neck, it sort of got me in check.You looked like something was wrong after and I asked if you were okay, you smiled with those space eyes with the little stars that light up when you laugh and said you're okay, but I should have known you weren't here to stay. I fell in love first and now my heart hurts after pouring it out over a boy who lied to me about his love. I am not a man yet. I am still at just a boy but you didn't look at it like that. You played my heart like a toy.

Hidden reality

I'm not saying I don't want to be here I don't want to be by myself, our self turns into himself for he is lost in his illusion an illusion of this never-ending oneself for one person, there is no plural of person to people of this illusion that's a hidden reality. Across misconception, they try to find a connection. Everything is connected but there are gaps within the connections which form misconceptions about him and to who he is. He tries to stay, but his illusion isn't so well erased for him it has a face, one that stares back at him in the middle of the night where he looks down and tells himself to fight. eyes see body but soul sees heart, that sort of is a piece of art everyone sees themselves only a silhouette of a person around their illusion. A never-ending oneself for one person.

Loves shove

Love is like a pinky promise. A bond formed at first touch. When you look in their eyes and they're looking back with their soul and you feel your heart as whole. Well me I lose all feeling, but not like I have before everything stops, and then it's all at once The Big Bang or rebirth as some call it. I try to lose my walls, some people are horrible and treat you like dirt, then the fear reinserts and you forget how to love, but sometimes people come along and give you a shove showing you how again to once love. My pinky promise was broken, my pinky promise was fake, I realized it wasn't me, but others who made the mistake. Then came along someone who gave me a shove and showed me how to once again love. I hope I stay above no matter the love.

Monster

A monster lives here, a monster lives within, a monster on my skin. Swords to fight through the night, a knife to remind them of their life. No sparkles to shine or fairies to fly for they are to die in the middle of the night, a knife to fight. A monster within, although you can see which ones flow deeper he's for sure creeper. Sometimes he's just like her, self-destruction in the eye of construction. Although you can see, but to what point of degree? A monster lives here, a monster within, a monster on my skin. To what point did it begin?

What's the difference?

I want something white, something bright, something only found in light. Color you see, color, let it be. For there is no color in light, something bright people to be full of sight. What is there in sight that it's so bright it can only be found in light? That's the message color you see, color let it be. Colors seen in the eye, color in the sky. What's the difference between a person and the sky? There is no difference, he says he is the sky; beautiful and bright, full of light. Color you see, color let it be.

Warm sun

Everything just stops. The world doesn't spin, I don't win. Have you ever seen a sand timer? From the outside, everything seems to be moving fast and making a lot of progress, but on the inside is what most people don't see; crawling through a narrow hole just trying to make your way out to the other side. I wish I knew why they all lied. Depression really isn't what most people think most days I'm on a boat just floating until I sink. Why did you sink? Well, you see, most people don't think. I lay on the boat feeling the warmth of the sun as it sinks, the waves of blood rocking me back and forth till I sleep, hoping my soul is to keep.

A choice

Life is in chapters. You become an adapter. For me well, I spent each chapter in laughter. Every day you have a choice, one of which you choose; laugh and adapt or make your own path. When you adapt, it gets hard to laugh. Reassurance I find at best. Sometimes it's not easy to put your head at rest. People think, people blink, sometimes, a thought isn't as easy as most people think. There is laughter in each chapter. It's all in your choice how you control each thought, something to be taught.You have a choice each day, it's your choice to be okay. Make the most of what you got. Everything can be perceived by a thought.

Lines

We take our first breath inside a box. Society makes gender, it creates pretenders. Living outside of the pink and blue lines, something to your life it must define. I am not wrong for I am strong. I don't see the lines to who I am to confine at birth, I was assigned. Society gave me a color to define; I added my own outside of that line. Some people say it's ugly, others say it's art. Sometimes my heart just falls apart for the next canvas already colored soon to see the world without a thought just uttered, something they muttered under their breath; to who I'm soon to be at death.

Falling pieces

Repairing your heart someone made fall apart, hitting restart it's honestly the hardest part. Most of the time I just don't know what's true and in my head, I constantly have to review to see what you meant when you had my heart in your hands, I guess no matter what I do I just won't meet your demands. Everything is on repeat in the dark, remarks make scars and scars show stars of people who've made friends with the dark. I count my demons and tally my heart the one you made fall apart when I trusted you that's just something I can't do; especially to you, but to anybody.

Try your "best"

What if this is my suicide letter, a hope things will eventually get better. Blue hair, black hoodie with the hood always up trying to disappear. You don't think I do but I always hear. I hear the screams, the smiles, everything as it piles. People look at you and expect a smile, I've been waiting for one for a while. Why is this my life; my wrist thinks of a knife. An endless pit in the bottom of my chest. I hope one day I'll be able to lay my head at rest, but for now, all I can do is try my best.

The 2nd

Whispered to me in silence, what do you hide? Tell me, when did you die? We all have our secrets to when we confide for me, it happened when I died. She looks at me through the mirror, a glass that couldn't be more clear.

Prominently

Rock bottom has a basement. I'm a misplacement. There's tornadoes of words in my head that I can't understand. I try to stand on both of my feet, which leads up bringing me to my knees as I weep. I'm not saying there's nothing but evil it just shows more prominently than the good. It creeps into your head and into your heart you may not know it, but I do; I know that I am smart and a work in progress is a piece of art. There's a tornado inside of me and that's the best way I could describe it. Everything's swirls around in a massive storm and you try to picture what was once there as the canvas just feels more and more bare. I make amends with my past every day. I see their reflection, I'm not sure if it's me, but I ask myself what it can be? I've lost all for what I've gained.

Bliss

Ethereal and movement I stare in their gaze, everything blurs out on a haze. Their hair a mist, a kiss at bliss. Can life be so beautiful I ponder, I stare as I wander; into the abyss while my heart floats into the mist.

Internal workings

I want someone to talk to. I want to be included. I want to be loved, but I don't. I don't have the energy anymore. I've been battling a war; my head against my heart. It's hard to look at yourself as art when you're falling apart. I put myself together in the eyes of society when mentally I'm battling my sobriety and the shell of my body I call anxiety. I see the world in a different view of which my mind drew, what would one hold to see the future? Would I be stronger or weaker, scared or brave? I don't think I'll know until I'm in my grave.

"Not so future message"

I have a message for myself, a message you need to hear now I know you might not listen but the end is not near. Although you may not hear as you're buried under invisible rocks and worried about clocks but please do note don't let me float. There's more to this life than beyond the handcuffs of your bedsheets and that damn door you always keep shut thinking about if you really want to cut. You may not listen with those songs on blast, but I can tell you not everything will last; that goes for both the good and the bad. One day, I hope you won't be so sad and learn that not everything can be bad. I know you're mad, and that's only because you're sad. It won't be about what you had, but what you have, you may not see the light, but you are your own. Remember, you are not alone.

What's beauty?

I ask myself what's wrong with me as I sit in the corner of my room, tears running down my face. What's wrong? You have to stay strong. It's screaming in my head you need to be fed, I know, I know. Pretty isn't defined as in the eyes of the beholder but within the eyes of society that affect the beholder. Yesterday I gave my ghost face, she held her arms out as a brace. She asked me what's wrong as she bled I told her I'm full of dread and I've been misled. Beauty has multiple definitions don't forget that when you look in the mirror. To your soul, you must hear.

Glass wall

A soul of a glass window. What happens if you look through? Isn't it what you already knew? A see-through soul is what most call but is it really see-through? Are you able to see why a person is mean? Maybe it's because they fall in between. They don't know when to be nice because people took advantage of them for that in more ways than one so they put on a tough front. Most people assume they're mean, but really, it's because they fall in between. A see-through wall that's not so see-through. It's not what you thought you knew.

It's not money

I'm as rich as all I can be with the smile you gave me. Who am I to be? A man of riches but not of money, something far more greater than anyone could wish for. They gave me happiness, something of which I was poor, it opened many doors, the first being my heart. That's where it all starts. I may not be rich of money, but I am rich as something else, something far more greater than anyone could wish for. I have happiness and that's all I ever need.

About the Author

At only seventeen Arrow Brake is the poet, writer, and author of the new novel "What we turned into" he is also the producer, podcaster, and designer of A.B.A.B. You can find his podcast (A.B.A.B.) on Spotify or wherever you get your podcasts you can also find his online store on his business Instagram page at a.b.a.b_designs or by googling redsunflowerjeep.wixsite.com